A Beginner's Guide to Demonic Possession & Exorcism

C.Z. Lazarus

Published by C.Z. Lazarus, 2021.

A BEGINNER'S GUIDE TO DEMONIC POSSESSION & EXORCISM

First edition. June 14, 2021.

ISBN: 979-8201375539

Written by C.Z. Lazarus.

Also by C.Z. Lazarus

Spirituality Over Suicidal Depression
The Interactive Book of Magic for Beginners
Energy Ball Bible
Control the Fire Element with Your Mind
You are the Magic Wand
Basic Pendulum Magic for Divination
Dark Energy Mastery Manual
Christos Magick
Enochian Handbook on Dark Wizardry
The Secret Seal of Solomon, Clavicula Magus
Energy Harmony Magic
Starsoul Wizardry Handbook
Reconstructing the Mind for True Spirituality
Arcane Magic for Beginners
The Psychic Witch Handbook
Cast a Magic Circle
A Beginner's Guide to Demonic Possession & Exorcism

Table of Contents

Overview 1

Is Possession Real? 3

Do Not be Afraid 7

Signs of Demonic Possession 9

Basic Defenses 15

4 Stages of Demonic Possession 21

Exorcism Techniques 25

How to Get the Name of the Demon 37

Safety Measures 39

Tips 47

A Message 51

For Anne M.

Overview

A Beginner's Guide to Demonic Possession & Exorcism is a spiritual manual that teaches the ins and outs of demonic possession, as well as how you can exorcise demons and other mischievous spirits/entities. This handbook will also teach you how you can protect yourself from psychic attacks and demonic infestations.

Demonic possession is real, and we are in a time when exorcism is necessary, for many are now possessed and manipulated by the evil ones without being aware of it.

It should be noted that denying the existence of evil does not deny their actual existence and their works in this world. In fact, to believe that demons and diabolical beings do not exist only strengthens them, for it allows them to do their works without detection. This makes them invisible and even more powerful.

A Beginner's Guide to Demonic Possession & Exorcism deals with the hard facts and reveals what has to be known. This handbook will give you the foundation that you need to be able to exorcise demons and diabolical beings. When it comes to real and actual exorcism, you need to be armed with the right foundational knowledge and practice. Do not forget the fact that you will be battling against true evil. Indeed, an exorcism is not something to be taken lightly.

Whether you want to free yourself, a loved one, or any other person from being possessed by an evil spirit, may the teachings in this handbook show you the light. You will be trained spiritually, and you will be prepared to deal with the enemy.

Be strong, have courage, and always remember that you are not alone. Just as there are demons and mischievous spirits out there, there are also angels and many other heavenly beings that come to our help. And, of course, there is God, the Divine Source, the Redeemer, and the Savior.

Are you ready to be trained and become an exorcist? If yes, then let me now welcome you into the world of spirits, good and evil, angels and demons, doubts, faith, love, and God.

Is Possession Real?

This is something that many people ask even today. There are those who believe that demonic possession is real, while others believe that cases of possession are mere medical problems without any spiritual or demonic significance. So, is possession real?

Those who deny the reality of possession are usually also the ones who deny the existence of the spiritual -—and sometimes, even the very existence of God, the angels, and all other spiritual beings. They are often materialists who succumb to the physical world and limit their life to it.

Today, many people quickly dismiss happenings of demonic possession as a mere mental problem, even without looking closely into a case. Indeed, there are many false cases of possession -—just as there are also many cases of what seemingly are mere mental illnesses but are actually caused by demonic infestation or possession.

However, it should be noted that there are signs that we can identify if a certain occurrence is a mere mental problem or a true case of demonic possession. Demons and other diabolical beings are so powerful that they leave traces that can help us know what is really happening -—but the exorcist needs to know where to look and what to find. A good example of this is the supernatural abilities that may be revealed by the one who is possessed, such as knowing things that should be outside their knowledge in normal circumstances, as well as being able to speak foreign languages unknown to the person who is possessed, among others. Demons are powerful, and it is often hard for them to hide the extent of their power.

It is also worth noting that many people who become possessed seek the help of several medical professionals first before they seek spiritual help. In fact, it is because medical assistance could not cure them that they end up in the hands of a priest, pastor, shaman, or any other spiritual person to undergo an exorcism.

An interesting case on this matter is the case of Anneliese Michel. Despite the people who claim it to be a simple case of mental illness, there are strong proofs that it was a real case of demonic possession. A closer look on the subject would reveal that the scientific bases are clearly insufficient to justify the conclusion of a simple mental problem or any other problem that merely relates to the human body. Indeed, in that particular case, demonic presence was as certain as daylight. Sadly, things did not go well for the young woman, but let us hope that her soul has now found peace with the Divine.

Before performing an exorcism, it has become a rule that the exorcist must first rule out all possibilities of mere mental or biological problems that should be in the hands of medical professionals. The problem with this approach is that it is very hard to rule out medical possibilities, also considering the fact that medical science always wants to give answers and explanations to everything and simply would not accept the truth that there are things that are simply beyond it, such as cases of demonic possessions.

Whether you believe in demonic possession is something that is up to you to decide. Needless to say, an exorcist is someone who believes in demonic possession. Personally, I can say that there are more reasons to believe in the existence of demons and bad spirits thereby giving way for possessions to occur than reasons to believe in them being false. Again, this is something that is up to you to decide.

Do Not be Afraid

A true exorcist must not be afraid of the demon or any other being that they are exorcising. Evil spirits feed on fear, which means that fear only makes them stronger.

However, it is difficult not to be afraid of demons. In fact, it is only reasonable to fear them. If we rely on human power alone, there is no definitely no way for us to win against a demon. But, if we have faith — faith in God — and if we have a good level of spirituality, then there is a way for us to win and free someone from demonic oppression.

Instead of fear, we should have faith. Now, this faith is not something that we develop just overnight. We develop it as we grow on the spiritual path.

To fear a demon is to allow ourselves to be overcome by it. However, we cannot fake real courage. It is either we have the courage (and hopefully enough courage) or we do not. Indeed, an exorcism is a real challenge, but in case of possession, there are times when an exorcism is the only way to save a life.

But how does one conquer this fear of demons? For man alone, this may be impossible, but we should realize that with God, nothing is impossible. Even if one were to be surrounded by a thousand demons, one may not fear as long as he/she is with God.

Therefore, it is necessary to cultivate one's spirituality. Now, it is very common for people to be afraid of spirits (not necessarily demons). Many of us are afraid of those that we do not understand. However, this fear of spirits is groundless once you realize that there is no reason to be afraid. There is one thing that you must realize: you are also a spirit.

Therefore, there is no good reason for you to be afraid of another spirit. Indeed, you have a body, but it is not you. You are a spirit, and your spirit is always connected to the Divine Source (God).

Signs of Demonic Possession

There are no hard and fast rules on demonic possession, but the following signs may help you detect if a possession is the work of a demon:

Aversion or Violent Reactions to Holy Objects

A common sign of demonic possession is if the victim demonstrates aversion or violent reactions to holy objects. The said holy objects may include the crucifix, Rosary, the Bible, holy water, and all other things that are connected to divine spirituality.

The way I like to do this is to secretly place the holy object somewhere where the physical senses would not be able to detect it. This is also a good way to find out if the victim is truly possessed or simply faking it. For example, you can secretly place a blessed Rosary under the seat where the victim will be seated. Watch for signs if the victim is feeling uncomfortable.

You can also do this openly by sprinkling holy water upon the victim and placing a crucifix on their forehead while you chant holy prayers.

Demonic and diabolical spirits would find it hard to stand the presence of holy objects because their energy would not be in harmony with the said objects. It would be like a war between two directly opposing forces.

Supernatural Powers

This is something that I really look for when I study a case of exorcism. Demons are powerful, and more often than not, victims of real possessions display supernatural abilities, such as the ability to read minds, know things about other people, levitation, and even the ability to move objects with their mind, among others.

This is not something that you need to compel them to do, but it is something that they would reveal as you go about the exorcism. Sometimes, these things manifest even prior to an exorcism. Be sure to watch out for these signs if you think someone is possessed by a demon.

Physical Changes and Disfigurations

Possessions can also manifest through physical changes like a change in eye color and other significant changes. The body may also appear to be disfigured. Disfiguration usually happens when the demon forces itself into the body of the victim while, at the same time, the exorcist and/or the victim try to fight against it.

Foaming in the Mouth

Foaming in the mouth is also a common sign of possession, especially when it appears that it happens naturally without the victim forcing it to happen.

Change in Temperature

Another sign of demonic presence is a drop in temperature. If you are facing someone who is possessed, you may feel the room getting cold. However, this is not a strict rule as it is also possible for the demon to do it the other way around and increase the temperature. However, most of the time, you can expect that the temperature will drop, thereby causing a colder temperature than normal.

Strange Smell

Among many cases of exorcisms, there have been reports of a strange smell either from the victim themselves or the room where they are in. The smell may vary, but many report a sulfuric kind of smell. Some claim that the smell of sulfur is like how hell smells like. Rotten and foul smells are also normal if you are facing someone who is possessed.

Ability to Speak in a Strange or Foreign Language

This sign is nothing new and is even shown in pop culture. This is where the person who is possessed is able to speak in a strange or foreign language that should be unknown to the victim under normal circumstances. Latin is also a language that is often attributed to cases of demonic possessions, but other foreign languages can also be observed. It is worth noting that the demons follow no rules except the objective to torture and cause detriment to the soul of the victim.

Howling and Any Other Animal-Like Signs

You should also watch out for animal-like behavior and sounds. A common behavior disclosed in many cases of exorcism is the victim creating howling sounds. The sound would be different from how a normal being would do it. The howl often appears to be unearthly, which is why it is easy to identify that it is coming from a demon.

Uneasiness

You may also notice a sense of uneasiness in the victim as you start to do the exorcism. This is the demon reacting to your exorcism. It will do its best to stay in the body of the victim, thereby causing so much uneasiness. You may notice the person to be possessed to be restlessly moving. The more that you exorcise the demon the more uneasy it will behave

Lying

Demons often lie. Take note that they do not always lie. They intentionally say the truth in some respects so that you will not know when they are finally telling a lie. Be careful when you deal with demons for they are expert liars.

However, a real victim of demonic possession would not want to lie about anything, for they badly need help. Hence, if you spot that the victim is lying to some of your questions, then there is a good chance that it is actually the manifestation of a demon at work.

Mind Tricks

Demons are highly intelligent beings. They are very good at tricking the mind. Hence, be careful about this. Watch out how the demons communicate to you. As an exorcist, always remember that you should be the one who is in control of the conversation and what is happening during the actual exorcism.

Do not let the demon trick you. A common tool they use is giving provocation. A demon may provoke you to think about something else so that you would not be able to focus on the actual exorcism. They will try to dominate your mind. As an exorcist, you must not let this happen. Instead, you should focus on what needs to be done. Stay calm and do what you must.

Erratic Behavior

You should also watch out for erratic behavior. This usually happens when the soul of the victim is fighting against the demon. This can also happen whenever you attempt to exorcise the evil spirit and the demon forces itself to stay in the body of the victim. Hence, as the body becomes confused, it may display erratic behavior.

Superhuman Strength

A common sign of demonic possession is where the victim demonstrates superhuman strength. Again, it should be emphasized that demons are powerful, and they often could not completely hide their power.

Important Note

There are no hard and fast rules on how to tell if a person is truly possessed or not. Among true exorcists from various religions, it has become a common practice not to conclude that someone is possessed right away.

In fact, the conclusion that a person is possessed should be the last and final option. This is why in many cases of possession, medical help is first exhausted before resorting to any acts of actual exorcism.

Basic Defenses

As an exorcist, you need to learn basis defenses against demons. This is not actual exorcism but it is good to incorporate practical psychic defense methods to keep yourself safe. Let us discuss them one by one:

Prayer

Prayer works, especially if it is uttered by a man of faith. When it comes to demonic attacks, an exorcist actually depends on the Divine, and connects with Divinity through prayer.

It should be clarified that it is not the actual exorcist himself who exorcises the demons but God. The exorcist only acts as the vessel or medium through which an exorcism is done, but it is still God who does the real work.

As far as basic protection is concerned, prayer is a sure thing that you can do. Pray to God and even to the holy angels and saints to protect you. Take note that you do not worship the angels and saints, for worship only belongs to God.

Salt Technique

Salt has been used since ancient times as a tool of cleansing and repellant against negative energy. Salt is also employed in many exorcisms. There are various ways to do this. You can mix salt with water and sprinkle it on the victim. Another way to do this is to place salt on the floor in the shape of a circle, keeping the victim within the circle. This is usually employed while the victim is lying on the bed or sitting on a chair. Remember that salt is a cleansing agent. It can help remove negative energy.

However, do not think that salt alone would be enough to get rid of a demon or a powerful evil entity. Salt can help but it cannot be a one-way solution. Its power is not enough to get rid of any demon.

Powder Technique

This is not a defensive technique but a helpful way to detect the presence of demonic spirits. For this technique, you will use a powder. The normal baby powder will work fine for this. You will place the powder on the floor. Ideally, you should have the victim sleeping on the bed. Place powder around the bed. Surround the bed with powder in such a way that you will have to step on the powder before any person can reach the bed where the victim is lying.

Leave the powder on the floor surrounding the bed overnight. In the morning, check for marks on the powder on the floor. If there is a demonic presence, there is a chance that you may see marks like coming from chicken feet on the floor.

Other marks resembling an animal may also be found. If you do not see any markings, then perhaps there are no demons at work, but there is still no 100% certainty. Hence, always be on guard and be careful.

Basic Psychic Shield

As an exorcist, it is also good to learn how to quickly protect yourself from negativity. This technique has been used by shamans and many occult practitioners for many years. It is a simple yet effective technique that you can use in an instant.

To form a basic psychic shield, simply imagine a bubble of white light around your body. Know that this shield shall protect you from all negativity and psychic attacks. See and feel it as clearly as you can. I like to imagine it as being made of pure white and divine light. The more that you can imagine it the more powerful it will be.

You can then go about with an exorcism or anything else that you may have to do. Take note that this instant shield does not last for a long time. On average, a psychic shield that is instantly created in this manner only lasts for a few minutes, about 5-10 minutes — or for as long as you hold the shield in your mind through imagination.

Just like any other magical skill, creating a powerful shield also takes time and practice. The more that you practice this technique the more effective you will be at casting it and the more that the life of the shield can be extended. Indeed, practice makes perfect.

Wearing Holy Objects

Holy objects hold power. It is not the physical attribute of the object anymore that matters but the energy that such object holds or represents. Wearing a holy object would automatically allow you to wear the specific energy quality that the object represents.

For example, by wearing a Rosary whether exposed or even in your pocket, you are able to wear the energy of that object. It may not be visible to people around you, but spirits and demons will be able to sense and even be affected by it. In a way, this works as a natural and easy way of protective magic.

If you are sensitive to energy, you can even scan a holy object and see how it makes you feel. Indeed, a holy object could be helpful to an exorcist when dealing with an evil entity.

Pure Heart

If you are serious about being an exorcist, then you should develop a clean and pure heart. No matter how hard you try and no matter how many prayers and psychic protections you have, if you possess an evil heart then there is no way you could win against a demon.

A true exorcist must have a pure heart. This is also another reason why a man can barely be an exorcist just overnight. You need to cleanse yourself, especially your heart. You should live a noble life and be free from sin and blame. Again, I repeat, if you want to be a true exorcist, then purity of heart is very important.

4 Stages of Demonic Possession

Through the years, demonic possession has been understood and given four stages or degrees. As an exorcist, you should know these stages so that you will have a good view of the case that you are handling. The four stages or degrees are infestation, oppression, obsession, and possession. Let us discuss them one by one:

Infestation

Infestation is not actual possession. This is merely the presence of a mischievous spirit. A good example of this would be what people refer to as haunted houses.

During this stage, a person is not yet being attacked directly. However, there will be signs of demonic presence, such as strange noises, foul smell, moving objects, and other unexplainable events. These things signify that something beyond the material world is at play.

It should be noted that manifestations of infestation do not always mean that a demon is involved, for it is possible that a different spirit (hopefully a good one) is also involved.

However, if it causes fear in a bad way or causes any kind of trouble, then there is a chance that you may be dealing with an evil spirit. Again, remember that in infestation, the spirit does not directly deal with a person but merely affects or makes itself manifest through objects or a place.

Oppression

The second stage is oppression. This time, a spirit would directly connect with a person — who will then be the victim. Here, manifestations of the spirit would be for the purpose of making its presence known to the person or even to cause fear to a person. Here, the spirit does not just deal with objects but primarily focuses on a person.

A good example of oppression is when the demon finally makes its presence known to the victim directly whether visually or by certain influence, such as causing the victim to have sleepless nights, unexplained fever, inducing fear, ghostly apparitions, and others. In this stage, the demon connects to the victim on a personal level.

Obsession

This stage is similar to possession, but it is of a higher level. Here, the demon becomes more manifest. When this stage is reached, the victim becomes more oppressed and a stronger link is made between the victim and the demon.

The victim will now experience direct attacks from the demon. With just a little more push, this stage will surely lead to a full-blown demonic possession.

Possession

Finally, the last stage is the actual possession of the victim by the demon. When it comes to possession, it should be noted that there are two schools of thought: One school of thought believes in the actual possession of the demon whereby the demon enters the body of the victim and takes control of it.

Another school of thought says that there is no literal possession or entry of the demon into the body of the victim. Rather, the demon is able to form a very strong link or connection with the victim, allowing the demon to take control of the victim. Just as no matter can occupy the same space at the same time, this school of thought believes that no two spirits can occupy the same body at the same time.

Regardless whether you believe the one or the other school of thought, the fact remains that the victim ends up being tormented and controlled by a demon and therefore needs to undergo a real exorcism.

It is also well to note that true possession only takes place in the last stage. However, an exorcism can be made regardless of the stage the victim may be in.

You do not need to wait for the demon to reach the final stage. In fact, the earlier that an exorcism is made the better, since the severity of the demonic attack tend to increase as you move up the aforesaid stages.

Exorcism Techniques

There are no hard and fast rules on how exorcism ought to be made. Over the years, various traditions and styles have been developed by different sects and groups.

You should understand that in a real exorcism, you are dealing with a living being — and not only that, since you are dealing with a demon, know that it is something that is highly intelligent and powerful.

Since you are dealing with a spirit that is very much alive and can think, you need to learn to adjust as the need arises.

As you exorcise the demon, you should pay attention to how it responds to whatever you do. Never forge that a demon will do its best not to be driven away from the body that it is possessing. It will not hesitate to use all its power to claim the body (and the life) of the victim that it is possessing.

Having said that, let us now discuss various techniques of exorcism that you can use to expel a demon and hopefully save a life:

Prayer

Perhaps the most common way of exorcism is by prayer. This has become commonplace as people see in many horror movies where a family calls for the help of a priest to help exorcise a demon out of the body of a loved one.

Catholics have a special book guide for exorcisms, but you cannot find the said book in the marketplace or in any public library. The book is only given to authorized persons within the Catholic Church.

In the Catholic Church, only a select few are allowed to exercise the power of exorcism. However, it should be noted that in ancient times, all people could practice exorcism. However, today, the Catholic Church does not allow just anybody to do it. This is also for a good reason since the practice of exorcism is not that easy.

You need to have the right knowledge and training before you can ever have a chance to win over a demon. Hence, the stand of the Catholic Church to only allow a select few to administer exorcism is also reasonable.

But, we all have the power to pray — and as according to the words of Jesus who, during His time on Earth also successfully exorcised demons, what is impossible for man is possible with God.

When we pray, we can ask the Lord Jesus Christ to exorcise the demon and the victim from oppression. Take note that we ought to ask in faith and not in doubt.

Hence, it is a requirement that one who wants to be an exorcist must develop their personal spiritual life; otherwise, they would never stand a chance against a demon.

Magic Circle

If you are into witchcraft, you might want to use a magic circle to help drive out the demon from the possessed. Now, there are many ways to cast a magic circle. A simple and effective way to do it is by placing salt on the floor in the shape of a circle. It should be big enough to surround the victim. You can also draw a pentacle inside the circle.

It is also advisable to have the victim in bed and surround the bed with salt. Take note that this is only the physical representation of the circle, but casting a magic circle does not end here.

The next important step is to call on the four mighty elements, also known as the guardians of the watchtowers. These elements are fire, water, air, and earth. Take note that elements refer to the four holy watchtowers or guardians of the universe. They are alive.

To call upon the elements, you should face the respective direction and call upon the elements one by one. You may need to use a compass for this. The directions of the elements are the following: south - fire, east - air, north - earth, and west - water.

As you call the elements one by one, see and feel the elements coming to you and joining you in the circle. Use your imagination. This is an effective and magical way of casting a magic circle.

You can then ask help from the mighty elements of nature to help you exorcise the demon. I have to say that this is not an effective approach unless you are a trained witch or sorcerer.

If you are someone who does not know anything much about magic, then it is best to use a different approach as this technique requires some degree of magical development.

Spellcasting

Witches and wizards rely on spells to drive away a demon. Now, there are many ways that one can cast for exorcism, but there is no one sure way to do it.

In exorcism, the ancients recommended to use the power of white light, believing that white light emanates from the Divine and that demons could not withstand it.

A simple way to do this is to imagine a ray of white light descending from heaven. See and feel as this white light enters the body of the victim. Let the white light fill the body and entire being of the victim.

Be confident of the fact that the light will heal the victim and drive away all negative energy, including any and all demons that may have connected themselves to the victim.

If you know the demon of the demon who is possessing the victim, you may write the name of the demon six times on a piece of paper.

You should then burn the paper in front of the victim, believing that by doing so you are also removing all links that the demon may have with the victim.

To competently use this technique, you should at least have a decent training in the practice of casting spells; otherwise, it would be better to resort to other techniques.

When you cast a spell, regardless of the spell that you cast, you should truly believe in it. Take note that doubt is a sign of weakness, and it will only empower the demon. Demons can feed on fear and doubts and this makes them stronger in the process.

Another helpful spell to cast is to visualize your guardian angel sending you their energy as you go through the exorcism process. It does not matter how you imagine your angel.

Angels can take all forms for they are pure spirit. The important thing is to know and believe that it is your guardian angel. There are those who go so far as to see and feel their angel being the one casting out the demon.

Indeed, there are many magical techniques that can be employed to exorcise a demon. However, the use of magic takes practice before you can employ it effectively. Therefore, if this is the technique that you intend to master, then you should start your magical training right now.

With the Help of the Victim

The victim can also help in the process of exorcism. If the victim would be able to do it safely (considering their health status), then it is good to have them engage in fasting. Water fasting would be recommended. The victim should also pray as much as they can.

Praying of the Rosary has also been recorded to be very effective. In fact, it is possible to drive out a demon by one's efforts simply by praying the Rosary. It is well to note that the Rosary is not limited to the Catholic Church, but anyone can pray it and enjoy its many benefits, such as healing and divine protection.

The victim should also not surrender to the demon. It is also possible for the demon to seduce a victim, and it is up to the person being possessed to fight against the temptation. Indeed, demons can be very tricky, but if the victim remains strong and holds on to the Divine, then there is a good chance that they can be free from demonic oppression.

The victim should also be open and honest to the one who is doing the exorcism. Both the victim and the exorcist should help each other to help achieve a common goal, which is the freeing of the victim from demonic possession and oppression.

Using Holy Names

Names have power. Hence, in an actual exorcism, the use of holy names has become a common and effective practice. Calling upon the names of Jesus and the holy angels and saints have been proven to be effective in exorcising a demon. Needless to say, this is something that has to be done in the spirit of faith. As such, anyone who wishes to be an exorcist must be a man/woman of prayer and faith.

By Command

When you exorcise a demon, you cannot be too kind. You should show the demon that you have full authority. The way to do this is not to ask the demon to leave but to actually command the demon to leave the victim.

However, just doing so under your own name might seem like nothing but a joke for a powerful demon. As such, it has become a common practice to exorcise a demon in the name of God.

Hence, we often hear exorcists say, "In the name of Jesus Christ," followed by a certain command to leave the victim. You can also use this technique, but make sure that you have a good relationship with Jesus.

Of course, if you are not a Christian, then you may use the name of the God that you believe in. Still, it is worth noting that throughout history, many demons have been expelled and successfully exorcised in the holy name of Jesus.

It should be noted that the command must be made in the name of God. A demon would not obey the command if it knows that the command is only given by a human being.

Demons know very well that they are more powerful than humans. Hence, when you give a command, do so in the name of God.

The best way to command a demon is to command it in the name of God and by its name. Take note of two important things: First, it should be in the name of God. Second, command the demon using its name.

Names hold power. If you learn the name of the demon, you can exercise over it by using its name. For example, let us say that the demon's name is Belial, then you would say, "In the name of Jesus Christ, I command you, Belial, to leave this woman/man." Feel free to use other statements. Here is another example, "In the name of Jesus of Nazareth, the Lord commands you to leave. Leave, Belial, leave!" You must give the command with faith and confidence in the Lord.

The Very Risky Approach (Not Recommended)

This approach is not recommended as this approach includes imposing some suffering on the victim, such as kneeling for hours, long periods of fasting, and some would even go so far as to inflict self-injury.

This approach tries to make the demon stop desiring the body of the victim, with a hope that the demon would find the body undesirable and leave it. However, demons know that these things are done exactly for that purpose, and so demons may choose to be patient and just wait it out.

A problem with this approach is that it causes so much discomfort and suffering on the victim, and it may even lead to death. Therefore, if you are going to use this approach, be very careful, and be very careful with the health and wellbeing of the victim.

Through the Reading of Sacred Scriptures and Holy Prayers

Reading sacred scriptures and holy prayers would make the demon feel very uneasy as its energy would find them highly undesirable. Hence, depending on your spirituality, you can resort to reading sacred scriptures and prayers. If you are a Catholic, the *Our Father*, *Hail Mary*, *Glory Be*, and *Psalm 23*, among others, are often used. Read and pray with faith.

The Rosary

So much can be said about the Rosary. Many miracles have been attributed to the Rosary, and for good reasons. Indeed, the Rosary is very powerful. In fact, there are real-world examples of demons being exorcised simply through the Rosary.

There are two main ways of using the Rosary for exorcism: You can pray the Rosary, and you can also put it around the neck of the victim. I suggest that you do both. Place a Rosary around the neck of the victim and pray the Rosary at the same time.

Still, it is important that the exorcist should be a man/woman of faith. Therefore, anyone who wishes to be a real exorcist must work on their spiritual development.

Do Whatever It Takes

As you gain more experience as an exorcist, you will realize that there are really no hard and fast rules on exorcising a demon. Many times, you just have to do whatever it may take to save a life.

Whatever it is that you must do would depend on the attending circumstances of a case. Pay attention to how the demon responds and find out its weakness.

Should you harness the victim?

In an exorcism, it is a common practice to harness the victim. This is because the demon can be very agitated and angry by the process of exorcism.

Harnessing the victim would be for your safety, as well as for the safety of the victim, as well as any other people who may be present. Harnessing the victim will also help to lessen distractions so that you could focus more on the work at hand.

It is up to you if you want to harness the victim. It is good to do so to avoid possible complications. You can tie the hands and feet while the victim is lying in bed or sitting on a chair. If you are feeling confident, then perhaps you do not need to harness the victim. This is a matter of personal choice, but it is encouraged that you harness the victim before you begin an exorcism. It helps to make things simpler.

How to Get the Name of the Demon

Names hold power. Although it is possible to exorcise a demon even without knowing its name, there are simply very powerful demons out there that it would be very hard to exorcise it unless and until you learn its name. However, you simply cannot expect a demon to give its name to you that easily.

An effective way to get a demon's name is by command in the name of God. Here is an example: "The Lord Jesus Christ commands you — what is your name, demon?" Here is another example: "The Lord Jesus compels you to tell us your name."

The demon may not tell you its name but give certain clues, such as symbols or other hints that lead to its name. Be sure to pay close attention and examine the details very carefully.

You can expect the demon to be protective of its name as it knows that giving its name away would make it vulnerable. Indeed, it will not be easy to know the real name of the demon, but once you get it, the work of exorcism will be much easier.

It should be noted that a demon will not want to give you its name. Therefore, this means that you can only get the name of a demon if you either force or trick it to give you its name. The only effective way to force a demon to give you its name is to command it to do so in the name of God.

Now, to trick a demon to give you its name is not easy to do as demons are very intelligent, and they are masters of trickery. But, what you can do is to offer an exchange. In exchange for its name, you can offer something that it may also like, such as a ritual offering of blood or fresh animal like chicken. Still, through history, it appears that the best way to get the name of the demon is through the use of commands in the name of God.

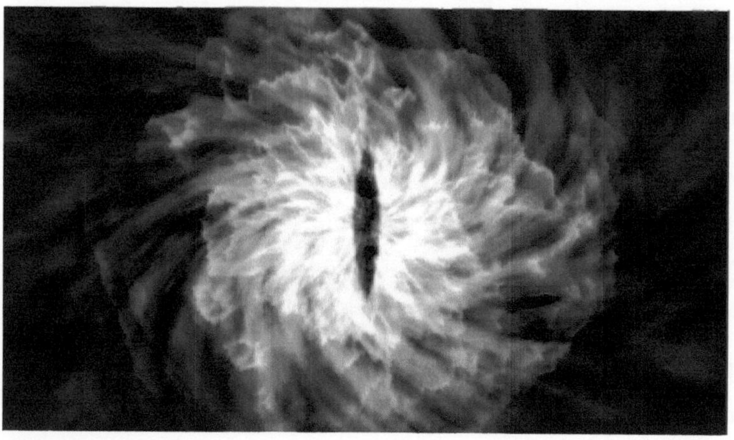

As an exorcist, you cannot limit yourself to just a single approach. You must be very open as it is hard to tell where things may go as the exorcism progresses. Never forget that you are dealing with a living, powerful, and intelligent being.

Safety Measures

Every exorcism is always a risky endeavor. In order to minimize the risk, you can observe some safety measures. It should be noted that no safety measures would guarantee a 100% safe exorcism, simply because an exorcism is always risky by nature as you will be fighting against a demon. Having said that, here are essential safety measures you should know:

Stay Calm

A true exorcist must never panic. If you panic and become afraid, the demon would know that it is the one in control of the situation. Needless to say, you can never let the demon be in control as it would never be well for any of you. A demon is only there to destroy and kill.

Although you are against a difficult adversary, you must stay calm at all times. In fact, unlike in the movies, you must avoid shouting. Shouting often signifies that you are not in control. Be peaceful, calm, and full of faith.

No matter what happens, do not let the demon notice that you are agitated or frustrated. Make the demon feel that you are in control. This confidence is not because you are powerful, but because you are one with God.

Have a Contingency Plan

You must always have a contingency plan. If you intend to do something but it does not work, do not panic. Instead, get to the next step (your contingency plan).

If nothing still happens, instead of becoming confused and showing the demon that you are losing hope, simply leave the room and come up with another tactic.

Record the Exorcism

This is not only a safety measure, but it is also strongly encouraged. You should record the whole exorcism session. Both video and audio recordings are recommended. This is also a good way to better understand a spirit.

It is also advised that you watch the recordings several times as they might help you find out something that you need to succeed. A good example of this would be signs or hints that you may have missed during the actual exorcism only for you to spot them as you watch the recordings.

Before you make any recordings, be sure to ask for permission first from the family of the victim. Explain to them its importance. Be sure to watch and keep a close eye on the recordings for they can reveal much about the demon.

Position cameras strategically in the room. Be sure to have the victim in full view at all times. It is good if you can take a clear view of the victim's face. Another good practice is to set up cameras and observe the victim overnight.

Take advantage of your recordings. It is not uncommon to watch them many times with a hope that they may give you some new insights.

Research

If the demon shows signs or gives strange messages, be sure to do a thorough research. If the victim writes something that may seem like a message, especially if it is a symbol, do a thorough research.

Gaining more knowledge can give you an advantage. The more that you understand the demon, the more that you will know how to best deal with it, as well as how to overcome it.

Thanks to technology, the Internet can be a great source of information. However, be cautious of the things that you read online. Do not believe in everything that you read right away. Be sure to check for reputable sources of information and use your common sense.

Do Not Do an Exorcism Alone

It is strongly suggested to do an exorcism with a group or at least with another person. Just be sure that the people who will be joining you in the exorcism are not too afraid, and they must have faith in God.

Before you proceed with the actual exorcism, it is good to educate those who will be participating in the exorcism. You do not need to explain everything, but at least let them know some simple ground rules, such as not panicking and focusing on the prayer.

If you ever find yourself in a situation where you need to do the exorcism on your own, just remember not to be afraid and to simply do your best.

Retreat

An exorcism is a war against demonic forces. You cannot expect for it to be easy. In a war, you cannot just always attack. You need to take precautions and be ready for whatever the other party may do. The same principle applies in an exorcism.

There are times when you need to keep pressing forward, but there are also times when you may need to retreat. The best time to retreat is when the demon is at its strongest. Many times, the best way to repel such an attack is simply to leave the room, and then return again once you have another plan in mind.

However, if you see that the life of the victim is highly at risk, then you must hold your ground and do your best. Pray fervently and do your best to save the victim.

Harness the Victim

It is always a good idea to keep the victim harnessed at all times during the exorcism in order to prevent the demon from causing more distractions. If you leave the victim unharnessed, there is a chance that physical attacks may be made by the demon.

When it comes to harnessing the victim, be sure to do it securely and safely. Take good care of the well-being of the person being harnessed. You do not need to cause any physical harm. If using a rope, be sure that it has a small texture to avoid hurting the victim. You can expect the spirit to use force and try to free itself, so be sure to tie the hands and feet properly and securely.

Team Up

The truth is that only a few people really understand how an exorcism works, and even fewer are those who have the training to perform a successful exorcism. If working on a case, it is strongly advised to team up with people who have actual experience in an exorcism and those who really know what they are doing. A team of at least three people would be ideal.

Avoid the Witching Hours

As much as possible, avoid performing an exorcism during witching hours (12AM & 3AM) as these times are believed to be moments when demons can exercise more power.

It is better if you can perform the exorcism during broad daylight. However, just because you do it during the day does not mean that the demon would be weak. Therefore, always be on your guard and exercise due diligence.

Do Not Rush

Exorcisms are not something that you would do in a hurry. Exorcisms usually take time. Although a single session of exorcism may do the job, it usually takes several sessions before you can make a demon completely leave the body of a person.

Therefore, when you engage in a case subject to exorcism, know that it will take lots of time — and you need this much time to defeat the demon. Use time to your advantage. Research, pray, and develop a strategy to beat the demon.

Remember That It is God Who is Exorcising the Demon

Although an exorcism may seem like a battle between you and the demon, the truth of the matter is that you shift the battle into the hands of God. This is why you command the demon to leave in the name of God — and the command also comes from God. You are merely a tool or medium that is used by God to send the demon away.

Unlike in the movies, a true exorcist must stay calm and keep their mind on God. When you talk to the demon, especially when giving a command, you do not need to be angry. Be calm and confident at the same time. Focus your mind on God and let the Divine Energy do the real work.

As you gain more knowledge and experience, you will learn other safety measures. Always keep an open mind and never stop learning.

Tips

- Do your best to get the name of the demon. Always remember that a demon's name is also its weakness. Once you know its name, you can more effectively command it to leave the victim.

- The number of demons that may be possessing the victim may also vary. It can be a single demon or even several demons at once. Find out how many demons are there and talk to them one by one. Be sure to expel all of them before you stop giving the rites of exorcism to the victim.

- A common trick used by demons is to make the exorcist think that they have already left even if they are still possessing the body of the victim. Again, watch out for signs and be vigilant. Do not forget that you are dealing with a spirit that is good at lying. Trickery is a part of their game. A good test to do is to make the victim pray the Rosary and read the holy scriptures out loud.

- You should not argue with the demon. You do not beat the demon through force but through the grace of God. Instead of arguing with the demon and becoming frustrated, you should focus on having more faith and understanding the demon and the victim.

- Although gaining more knowledge and understanding of what is happening may help, know that it is not important for you to understand everything. It is still the Divine action that will be the primary force that will drive out the demon.

- If in doubt, do not take any action. Instead, be still and pray.

- The demon will do its best to make you lose your focus. It will distract you from the things that you need to do. It can talk harshly to you or even say things that would provoke you to anger and cause you to lose your faith. Simply put, it will do all its best to weaken you spiritually and mentally, as well as emotionally. As an exorcist, you must not listen to the demon. You have been warned already, so do not be surprised if you encounter a demon who would do these things.

- Although it is considered important to know the name of the demon (or demons) to cast it out, it should be noted that it is still possible to have a successful exorcism even without knowing the name of the demon. Still, an exorcism would be more powerful and effective if you know the name of the demon.

- If the demon cannot be exorcised in just one session, do not hesitate to take a break. You also need to rest, as well as the people who will be helping you with the exorcism. Once you have enough strength, then you can return and have another round of exorcism.

A Message

By now, you should be equipped with the knowledge and practice that you need to be a real exorcist. Being an exorcist is not easy; you can expect many challenges and unexpected experiences along the way. Still, every time that you are able to help someone, the fact of being able to help alone is simply priceless.

It is important to emphasize that if you are serious about becoming a real exorcist, then you must develop your spirituality. Jesus was able to exorcise demons almost instantly without any techniques for He has a very high level of spirituality — after all, He is the Son of God, and even God Himself. We, as normal and sinful human beings, should exert more effort. But, let us not be discouraged, for what is impossible for man is possible with God. As long as we are with God, we shall fear no evil.

The beauty of being an exorcist is not only each time you engage in an actual session of exorcism, but the path itself is holy and full of spiritual life. The training to be a real exorcist requires that you draw close to the Divine. The path makes us spiritual. This is why real exorcists are not afraid of demons, for they are very close and dear to the Divine Light, Jesus.

Although this handbook has given you techniques, know that there are no hard and fast rules on exorcism as you are dealing with a real living being — and an evil one. As such, as an exorcist, we need to learn to adjust and trust in God. If we humble ourselves and let the Divine Energy fill our being, then the

Divine can use us as the medium to fight against the powers of darkness.

We now end our discussion with the wisdom of Saint Padre Pio: "Pray, hope, and don't worry."

Did you love *A Beginner's Guide to Demonic Possession & Exorcism*? Then you should read *The Interactive Book of Magic for Beginners*[1] by C.Z. Lazarus!

[2]

The Interactive Book of Magic for Beginners reveals the craft of magic and teaches it in an interesting and easy-to-understand manner, so that anyone can have the chance to learn and experience the beauty and power of magic.

The Interactive Book of Magic for Beginners presents magical characters, such as Orbus the green goblin, Mathilda the sweet and gentle sylph, Professor Juliet, and Professor Hedgar, among others. They will teach you the secrets of the craft of magic. With

1. https://books2read.com/u/baaYpQ

2. https://books2read.com/u/baaYpQ

their help, you will learn and understand the mysteries of the universe and be able to use the secrets of the craft to create real and positive changes in your life.

This book will give you the foundation that you need to learn and master the holy science and art of magic. You will learn essential theories and magical practices that will allow you to fully experience magic on a personal level. This is not a book that you read today and forget about tomorrow. Rather, this is a journey — a journey into a truly magical life. *Are you ready to take this journey? Are you ready to experience real magic in your life?*

For many years, countless people searched for genuine magical instructions, but their attempts often ended only in vain. This book has been written so that anyone who sincerely desires to learn the way of true magic may be given a chance to do so. The teachings in this book are based on legitimate and most genuine foundations of the craft of divine magic, which you can also verify not only through diligent research, but more importantly, through actual practice and personal experience.

Back in the Old Days, a time when humans lived in harmony with nature, magic was a natural part of the lives of the people. It was a beautiful time when humans, faeries, halflings, and many other magical creatures lived happily together, helping one another. Back then, even angels communicated directly with humans. Sadly, humanity started to fall as evil started to grow in their hearts, a corruption that was so dark and evil. We gradually lost touch of the magical world that was once our home. The fairies flew away from us, the legendary unicorns hid themselves from our sight, and all other magical creatures we used to love left us alone with our evil.

The Interactive Book of Magic for Beginners is a portal that will take you back into the realm of magic where you truly belong, where you can immerse yourself in the true teachings and ways of the sacred art of sorcery and witchcraft. If you desire for real magic, then this is for you. The good news is that magic is not completely lost. If you just open your heart and mind to it, then you will discover that it is as real today as it was thousands of years ago.

If you are ready, then come and join me on a wonderful journey of life, love, spirituality, and overflowing magic.

Also by C.Z. Lazarus

Spirituality Over Suicidal Depression
The Interactive Book of Magic for Beginners
Energy Ball Bible
Control the Fire Element with Your Mind
You are the Magic Wand
Basic Pendulum Magic for Divination
Dark Energy Mastery Manual
Christos Magick
Enochian Handbook on Dark Wizardry
The Secret Seal of Solomon, Clavicula Magus
Energy Harmony Magic
Starsoul Wizardry Handbook
Reconstructing the Mind for True Spirituality
Arcane Magic for Beginners
The Psychic Witch Handbook
Cast a Magic Circle
A Beginner's Guide to Demonic Possession & Exorcism

www.ingramcontent.com/pod-product-compliance
Ingram Content Group UK Ltd.
Pitfield, Milton Keynes, MK11 3LW, UK
UKHW040013200726
13854UKWH00001B/173

9 798201 375539